ELEANOR OF AQUITAINE

Convincing Beauty

THE HISTORY HOUR

HISTORY

"Now there stood before him the young, worldly and disturbingly beautiful Queen of France, intent upon meddling in matters that were not her concern."

— ALLISON WEIR, ELEANOR OF
AQUITAINE: A LIFE

CONTENTS

❧ I ❧
PROLOGUE

೫⁊೪

Eleanor of Aquitaine is the key person of the book. It goes without saying she was the most powerful of all queens of medieval France and England. She was born in 1122 to William X, Duke of Aquitaine and his wife Aenor de Châtellerault. Aquitaine was the largest (one-third the size of modern France) and richest province of those times.

೫⁊೪

Eleanor got the best education and became the outstanding conversationalist. Her mother and brother William Aigret died in 1130 and she became her father's heir.

೫⁊೪

In 1137 Duke William went on Pilgrimage and left his children with the Archbishop of Bordeaux. Before leaving Bordeaux, the duke dictated a will in which he left all of his lands to Eleanor, and he appointed King Louis VI of France as her guardian.

❧

The same year William died and the King of France, being in no better condition than Duke, arranged the marriage of his 17 year old son to 15 year old Eleanor. This meant Aquitaine went under total control of the crown of France.

❧

The couple had only two daughters and no sons. Eleanor was beautiful and high-spirited and could influence her husband Louis. While a Crusade Louis and Eleanor had an argument. The king wanted to go to Jerusalem as a pilgrim but Eleanor pressed for the army to attack the Muslim forces. That argument was fatal to their marriage. It was annulled.

❧

On May 18, 1152 Henry II and Eleanor married. They had 8 children with 5 boys among them. In 1167 the couple decided to separate.

❧

In 1173 Eleanor was imprisoned and only 17 years after she was set free. Eleanor died in her late 70s.

❧

The book tells you about bright events of the lives of her husbands and sons who left a mark in the history of Europe.

❧ II ❧
CHAPTER 1 – CHILDHOOD IN AQUITAINE

"Trees are not known by their leaves, nor even by their blossoms, but by their fruits."

— ELEANOR OF AQUITAINE

BIRTH OF AN HEIRESS

❧❧❧

In 1122, William X, Duke of Aquitaine, and his wife Aenor de Châtellerault, welcomed their first-born child. They named her Aliénor, from the Latin *alia Aenor,* meaning "the other Aenor." Through the years, and through the application of different languages, she came to be known as Eleanor.

❧❧❧

Duke William's Aquitaine was the largest and richest province in all of France. When combined with Poitou, the lands that Aenor had brought to her marriage, the family ruled over an area that was almost one-third the size of modern France. Aquitaine was a vassal dom of the kings of France but due to its size and power it was largely independent. The region was in possession of the wines of Bordeaux, which are still rightly famous; multiple sea ports gave access to trade that more land-locked regions desperately wanted; and the bustling and cosmopolitan cities of Bordeaux and La Rochelle were acknowledged centers of culture. It was a jewel.

⁂

Eleanor was given the best education that any child could receive. She spoke Poitevin, a regional dialect that still exists today, but she was able to read, write and converse in Latin. She was extensively tutored in mathematics, history, astronomy, music and literature. She learned how to hunt, hawk and ride as well as any man. She was also taught the "womanly" arts of household management, embroidery, needlepoint, spinning and weaving. She excelled in the social arts, learning to dance and play the games that were popular in court. She also became a witty and accomplished conversationalist, flirty and intelligent and more than a bit strong willed. She knew her mind, and she wasn't afraid to share her opinions. She would be known for the rest of her life for her fiery and independent spirit.

⁂

She was joined by two legitimate siblings, William Aigret and Patronilla. William X had a bastard son, Joscelin, who was acknowledged and made part of the family. They lived in Poitiers with their parents, close-knit and loving siblings who would remain close for the rest of their lives.

⁂

In 1130, William Aigret and her mother Aenor died in Talmont, one of the cities on Aquitaine's Atlantic coast. With the passing of her brother, Eleanor became the heir presumptive of her father's holdings, and the most eligible heiress in all of Europe.

HEIRESS, DUCHESS, QUEEN

❦

I n 1137, Duke William left Poiters and moved to Bordeaux, taking his children with him. When he reached the city, he left Eleanor, Petronilla and Joscelin in the care of the Archbishop of Bordeaux. In a time of increasing skullduggery and political intrigue, the archbishop was one of the few vassals that Duke William could trust.

❦

The Duke intended to go on pilgrimage, a common enough activity for the time, and he needed to leave his children with someone he could depend upon. He had reasons to be concerned – kidnapping heiresses and forcing them into marriage was a viable route to obtaining a title, and the worst of men could force themselves into the halls of power on the backs of unwilling brides. Before he left Bordeaux, William dictated a will in which he left all of his lands to Eleanor, and he appointed King Louis VI of France as her guardian. This meant that until the king had found a suitable husband for young Eleanor, Aquitaine and its possessions were in Louis' care. Legally, the king had the right to her lands, so kidnapping Eleanor would avail nothing to would-be dukes.

୧୫୨

The will was dictated perhaps with some foreknowledge on Duke William's part, for he fell desperately ill while he was on pilgrimage to the Shrine of Saint James of Compostela. He was aware that he was dying, and he told his companions to keep his death secret until King Louis and the archbishop could be informed. Duke William succumbed to his illness on Good Friday, 1137, making Eleanor the Duchess of Aquitaine.

୧୫୨

His retainers took the news to the king and the archbishop as quickly as they could. Unfortunately, King Louis was in no better shape than Duke William. When the Duke died, King Louis was suffering from a deadly bout of dysentery. He received the news of William's death with something like elation, for he had an unmarried son and namesake. He immediately arranged the marriage of the 15-year-old duchess to his 17-year-old son, bringing Aquitaine firmly under the control of the crown of France and the ruling House of Capet.

୧୫୨

Prince Louis was sent to Bordeaux with Abbot Suger, who was in charge of wedding arrangements, along with Raoul I,

Count of Vermandois and the seneschal of France; Count Theobald II of Champagne, son of Stephen, Duke of Blois, and the older brother of King Stephen of England; and an escort of 500 knights. The sight of such a nobly and manly entourage must have been inspiring to young Eleanor, who was always a romantic at heart. The young couple were wed on July 25, 1137, at the Cathedral of Saint-André in Bordeaux. They were immediately proclaimed Duke and Duchess of Aquitaine and Count and Countess of Poitou.

༺❀༻

The archbishop of Bordeaux performed the wedding ceremony, as well as one last service for his late liege lord: in negotiating the details of the marriage with Abbot Suger, the archbishop secured the agreement that the lands of Aquitaine would remain independent of France and the sole property of Eleanor until such time as her oldest son came of age and became both King of the Franks and Duke of Aquitaine. Only then would Aquitaine become merged with France.

༺❀༻

Eleanor gave Louis a wedding gift that can still be seen today. Called the Eleanor Vase, it is a rock crystal vase with gold details. Louis gave the vase to the Basilica of St. Denis, where it remained for centuries. It is on display at the Louvre and is the only item belonging to Eleanor that still remains in existence.

༺❀༻

Only days after the wedding, while Louis and Eleanor were

touring their shared provinces, news arrived in Bordeaux that Louis VI had died of dysentery on August 1, 1137. On Christmas day, 1137, Louis and Eleanor were crowned and anointed as King and Queen of the Franks. With her siblings in tow, the royal couple returned to Paris.

CHAPTER 2 – CONFLICT

"I thought I was wed to a king – now I find I am wed to a monk."

— ELEANOR OF AQUITAINE

CROWN VERSUS CROSS

❧❦❧

Eleanor was not well liked in Paris. She was too high-spirited for the demure and rigidly modest society there. She was opinionated and outspoken in a place and time when noblewomen were expected to be meek, humble, subservient and modest. She dressed with style and color, something that scandalized the staid court of the Capets. She was beautiful, worldly, and struck the noble circles of Paris like thunderclap. Church elders, especially Bernard of Clairvaux, took her to task for being "indecorous" and inappropriate.

❧❦❧

Louis, however, was besotted with his glamorous wife. He spared no expense to bring the Cité Palace of Paris more comfortable and more like the elegant home in Aquitaine she had left behind. He showered her with affection and gifts and gave in to her every whim. Eleanor made a game of seeing how far she could push him and how much he would give her, and she found that her new husband's generosity had no limits. It was no wonder that her mother-in-law, Adelaide of Maurienne, thought Eleanor was a bad influence.

❧

In this time period, there was a power struggle between the Vatican and the secular rulers of Europe regarding who had the right to appoint holders of important religious posts. The power struggle in France came to the fore in 1141 when the Archbishop of Bourges died, leaving the position open. Louis was a pious man, but he believed in the divine right of kings, and that this right extended to naming the bishops in his own lands, who would be his vassals as well as servants of the Church. He named one of his chancellors, Cadurc, to the post and refused to acknowledge Pierre de la Chartre, who was Pope Innocent II's pick for the archbishopric of Bourges.

❧

In rebellion against the king, the canons of Bourges elected Pierre, and he was consecrated by the Pope. Louis retaliated by barring the gates of Bourges against Pierre, preventing him from entering the city when he returned from Rome. The counts of Poitou had staged similar opposition to the Vatican in the past, so Innocent blamed Eleanor for the "outrage" and announced that Louis was a child who needed to be taught manners. Completely enraged, Louis swore upon relics that for as long as he was alive, he would never allow Pierre to enter Bourges. The Pope responded with an interdict on Louis' lands, a papal order that banned all residents of the affected areas from attending church or receiving sacred rites like confession, communion, marriage, baptism or even Christian burial. Pierre was given refuge by Theobald II of Champagne.

FAMILY FEUD

෨෪෨

I t was at this time that Raoul I of Vermandois sought King Louis' permission for him to repudiate his wife, Eléonore of Blois, sister of Theobald II of Champagne, in favor of Eleanor's sister, Petronilla of Aquitaine. Eleanor fully supported her sister's marriage to Raoul, since Petronilla and the seneschal had been involved in a torrid affair for quite some time. As always, Louis gave Eleanor anything she wanted, so he granted Raoul the right to put his wife aside. Raoul and Petronilla were wed.

෨෪෨

Unfortunately, in the eyes of the Church, Raoul and Eléonore were still married, which made Raoul a bigamist and Petronilla an adulteress. Theobald II took great umbrage at the insult to his sister, and he declared war on Louis. The war lasted for two years (1142 – 1144) and ended with the king's army occupying Champagne. At Eleanor's urging, Louis personally led his forces in an assault on the city of Vitry. A thousand people sought refuge in the church there, only to die when the royal army set the edifice ablaze. Horrified, Louis tried to make peace with Theobald in return for the count's assistance in lifting the interdict. Theobald agreed, and the interdict was lifted. Louis restored Theobald's lands to his control and retreated to Paris. No sooner had Louis returned to Paris than the Vatican ordered Raoul to repudiate Petronilla, which he refused to do. The interdict was lowered once again, with Theobald's urging, along with an excommunication for Raoul and Petronilla. Louis resumed the war.

❧

In June 1144, while Eleanor and Louis were visiting the newly-built monastery at St. Denis, the queen met with the abbot, Bernard of Clairvaux, and demanded that he exercise his influence with the Pope to have her sister's excommunication lifted. She told the cleric that if he did this, then Louis would withdraw from Champagne and recognize Pierre as the Archbishop of Bourges. Bernard upbraided her for her pride and for daring, as a woman, to interfere with matters of state.

❧

Surprisingly, Eleanor turned penitent and meek. She told Bernard that she was bitter because she had no children, and she begged him to forgive her behavior. The future saint responded warmly, telling her that if she would stop riling up Louis and egging him into rebelling against the Church, he would intercede with God and ask "the merciful Lord to grant you offspring." Peace was declared, Theobald's lands were restored, and Pierre was installed as archbishop.

In 1145, Eleanor gave birth to a daughter, Marie de France.

❧ IV ❧
CHAPTER 3 – PENITENT CRUSADE

"I dressed my maids as Amazons and rode bare-breasted halfway to Damascus. Louis had a seizure and I damn near died of windburn...but the troops were dazzled!"

— ELEANOR OF AQUITAINE (THE LION IN WINTER)

ELEANOR AT WAR

❧

Louis was still tortured by the fiery massacre in Vitry, and he declared an intention to go on pilgrimage to the Holy Land in atonement for this grievous sin. In the autumn of 1145, Pope Eugene III asked Louis to personally lead a Crusade to rescue the Crusader kingdoms there and to retake Edessa. The Crusader kingdom of Antioch was ruled by Prince Raymond, who was also Eleanor's beloved uncle. Louis agreed to take up the cross, and on Christmas Day 1145, he dedicated himself to the cause in the cathedral of Bourges.

❧

Eleanor took up the cross, herself, something of an anomaly for noble women. Further, she recruited many of her royal ladies in waiting and over 300 non-noble vassals and knights from Aquitaine to join the endeavor. She insisted on leading her vassals from the front, since she was the rightful feudal leader of her Aquitainian army. Per usual, Louis permitted it.

☙❧

Louis was as bad at disciplining an army as he was at refusing his wife. They were disorderly and disobedient, and they fell prey to stalling tactics implemented by Manuel I Comneneus, the Emperor of Byzantium. He feared that the Crusaders would upset the delicate balance of power in the region and jeopardize his kingdom's well-being, and he had some reason for his concern.

☙❧

Part of the Byzantine emperor's strategy to delay the Crusaders was to fête and celebrate Eleanor and Louis. The royal couple were housed in the Phlipation palace just outside the city walls, and they were treated to banquets and adoration. Eleanor, because of the cloth of gold that adorned the hem of her robe, was called *chrysopous* (golden-foot). Greek historian Nicetas Choniates compared her favorably with the mythical Amazon queen Penthesilea, and the people of Byzantium greatly admired her for her beauty and vivacious character. Louis and Eleanor were the toast of the town for three weeks.

☙❧

Manuel I Comneneus told Louis and Eleanor that German King Conrad had won a spectacular victory against the Turks, news that filled them with optimism for the retaking of Edessa and the defense of Antioch. Unfortunately, it was a lie. The German army had been massacred. Louis and Eleanor left Constantinople in high spirits, believing that the war was almost won.

⚜

Their army encamped near Nicea, and while they were there, the decimated remnants of Conrad's forces staggered into view. They were led by Konrad himself, who was ill and confused. They brought the news of their defeat, but they joined the French army for its increasingly scattered march on Antioch.

⚜

When the army camped near Ephesus, they were ambushed by the Turks, but they beat them back with such ferocity that they were able to take the Turkish army's camp in retaliation. Much buoyed by this success, they continued on their way.

⚜

Louis decided that the army should cross the Phrygian Mountains directly in order to reach Antioch more quickly, and in so doing, the French army discovered the grisly remains of the German army, its corpses left unburied and rotting in the field.

DISASTER STRIKES

❦

Louis and Eleanor led their forces over Mount Cadmos, with Eleanor and her Aquitainian knights led by Geoffrey de Rancon at the vanguard while Louis took command of the rear. The king, who was more and more dedicated to the Crusade as a pilgrimage rather than a military action, chose to dress in peasant clothes and ride with the unarmed pilgrims and baggage train that followed his army.

❦

The Turks followed them closely, harrying them with feints and keeping pace. They were watching for an opportunity, which was presented to them soon enough.

❦

Baggage and civilians move far slower than knights on horseback, and soon the Aquitainian contingent had pulled far ahead of the rest of the army. They reached the summit of Mount Cadmos and although Rancon had been instructed to make camp there, he decided to press on since much of the day remained. He was supported in this decision by Amadeus III, the County of Savoy, who was Louis' uncle. They decided to move on to a nearby plateau and make camp there, instead.

৩১৬৩

The baggage train, believing that they were nearing the end of their travel for the day, were taking their time. A gap opened in the army, with Eleanor and her knights already crossing the summit while the rest of the army was still approaching it. The Turks saw their chance and attacked. The French army and the pilgrims were trapped at the edge of a crevasse in the mountain, unable to run and unable to find room to really fight. Those who stood to fight were slaughtered, and many who tried to escape were caught and killed. Louis's bodyguards, who were distinguished from their companions by the royal crests on their garb, were all killed, their skulls bashed in and their limbs severed. Louis himself only survived by climbing the rock face using tree roots for handholds. Men, horses, and baggage were all flung down the crevasse to die.

৩১৬৩

Blame for the carnage was placed on Eleanor's shoulders, with historians like William of Tyre claiming that the reason was excessive baggage belonging to the queen and her ladies. Officially, Geoffrey de Rancon was blamed because of his failure to obey the orders he'd been given. There was some talk that he should be hanged, but Louis ignored that suggestion. As Eleanor's vassal, Geoffrey may have been following her orders when he did not stop to make camp, which ultimately led to the massacre. The split between the French and Aquitainian forces was certainly a factor in the defeat, and the fact that the forces from Aquitaine had avoided the attack entirely painted them all with the accusation of cowardice.

❦

As the army continued toward Antioch, the commoners marched overland while the royals sailed to the city. While they were en route, an argument arose between Eleanor and Louis. The king intended to go to Jerusalem as a pilgrim, which he had always stated was his purpose in going on Crusade. Eleanor, however, at the urging of her uncle Raymond, pressed instead for the French army to attack the Muslim forces encamped at Aleppo. A victory there would clear the way to retaking Edessa, which was the Pope's intention.

❦

The argument was fatal to their marriage. Rumors sprang up that Eleanor's insistence on holding to Raymond's plan – which was the more efficient military plan – was because she and her uncle were involved in an incestuous affair. These rumors, along with the accusation that Eleanor's excess baggage had been one of the causes for the French defeat, reached Europe and besmirched her reputation. Eleanor, aggrieved, brought up the question of consanguinity (the idea that Eleanor and Louis were too closely related by blood to be lawfully wed) and requested to be left at Antioch when Louis went to Jerusalem. Louis refused and forced her to accompany him and the rest of the army on the remainder of his pilgrimage.

⚜

Eleanor was infuriated and humiliated by Louis telling her "no" for the first time, and she sulked her way through the rest of the campaign. Louis, King Conrad and King Baldwin II of Jerusalem laid siege to Damascus in 1148 but accomplished nothing. The rulers of Jerusalem and Damascus had recently entered into a treaty, and by laying siege to the city, Baldwin and by extension Conrad and Louis were cast as oath-breakers, ruining their credibility among the Crusader orders who were to support them in combat. The siege ended in failure.

⚜

Disheartened by defeat, struggling through a long and under-supplied march to Jerusalem for Louis's pilgrimage, Eleanor and her Aquiatainian knights were demoralized. Her vassals no longer listened to Louis's orders. Neither did the French. The entire Crusade was a failure.

ANNULMENT

❧

Eleanor's "excessive affection" for her uncle Raymond grated on Louis's nerves, and the rumors took their toll. When it became clear that Raymond intended to abduct Eleanor (with her blessing), it was too much. It was time for Louis and Eleanor to return home to France. They did so, however, on separate ships, too at odds to even occupy the same vessel for the trip.

❧

In May 1149, the Byzantine navy attempted to seize the royal pair, but they managed to escape the attack with little damage. A storm blew up, however, and drove Eleanor's ship far off course, sending it to the Barbary Coast, many miles south of where she was meant to be. Louis had troubles himself, and neither of them were heard from for over two months.

⚜

Eleanor's ship finally limped into port in Palermo, in Sicily, where she learned that she and her husband had both been given up for dead. The King of Sicily, Roger II, welcomed her and gave her food and a place to stay. Finally, Louis and his ship appeared in Calabria, and she actually went to meet him there. The royal couple met up at King Roger's court at Potenza, where bad news was received from the holy land. Eleanor's uncle, Raymond of Antioch, had been captured and beheaded by the Muslim army. She was grief-stricken.

⚜

Instead of returning to France, Eleanor and Louis traveled instead to Tusculum, where Pope Eugene III was in residence. Eleanor broached the subject of consanguinity, which was one of the only grounds for annulment of marriage in the medieval world. The pope did not comply. Instead, he announced that no word could be spoken against the appropriateness of their marriage, and that it was not to be dissolved for any reason. He also manipulated her until she had no choice but to share a bed with her now-despised husband. A second child was conceived under these less than ideal circumstances, a daughter, Alix of France.

⚜

Louis was crushed. He had longed for a son, but instead his contentious wife had given him another daughter. Worse, in the wake of news of the disaster in the mountains, his barons were uniting against his wife. Eleanor was still pressing for annulment. With no son and in danger of being left with no male heir, the king at last acquiesced.

Louis and Eleanor traveled to the royal castle of Beaugency were, on March 11, 1152, they agreed to annul their marriage. The proceedings were presided over by Hugues de Toucy, Archbishop of Sens, and the Archbishop of Bordeaux and the Archbishop of Rouen represented the king. Archbishop Samson of Reims represented the queen. Pope Eugene granted the annulment on March 21, 1152, on the grounds of consanguinity within the fourth degree, because they were related as third cousins through Robert II of France. Their daughters were not bastardized, and custody was awarded to Louis. Archbishop Samson procured a pledge from Louis that Eleanor's lands would be returned to her, and the marriage ended.

❦ V ❦
CHAPTER 4 – A NEW KINGDOM

"In a world where Carpenters get resurrected, everything is possible."

— ELEANOR OF AQUITAINE

ENTANGLEMENTS IN
NORMANDY

❦

Eleanor traveled back to Poitiers after the annulment, and along the way she was beset by two different men who tried to abduct her and force her into marriage. One was Theobald V, Count of Blois, and the other was Geoffrey, Count of Nantes. She avoided both men, but when she reached her castle safely, she sent an envoy to Henry II, Duke of Normandy (Geoffrey of Nantes's brother) offering him her hand. He accepted. The two were wed only eight weeks after the annulment from Louis was completed, on May 18, 1152.

❦

They made an unlikely couple. It was rumored that Eleanor had had an affair with Geoffrey V, Count of Anjou, who was Henry II's father, and that Geoffrey had warned Henry away from her. Also, the two were even more closely related than Eleanor and Louis. She had shared one relative with Louis, but with Henry, she had three: Ermengarde of Anjou; Geoffrey, Count of Gâtinais; and King Robert II of France. In fact, Henry II and Eleanor's daughter Marie de France had been prohibited from marriage on the grounds of consanguinity.

৩১৩

The marriage was taken as an insult by Louis, who saw it as an intentional way for Henry II, who had long been Louis' rival, to prevent his daughters Marie and Alix from inheriting Aquitaine. With this marriage, Henry now controlled more French land than the King of France, which was untenable from Louis' point of view. He mobilized an army and marched on Normandy, which included forces under the command of Henry's own brother, Geoffrey. Meanwhile, in England, King Stephen (Henry's uncle) lay siege to a one of Henry's castles, trying to take advantage of Henry's French distractions to gain some ground in the civil war that was tearing England apart.

৩১৩

Henry was not one to be distracted, and he counter-attacked Louis and Geoffrey, pushing them back out of his lands. Louis fell ill and retreated back to Paris, and Geoffrey lost his main castle to Henry, who forced him to come to terms. With his brother humbled and his wife's ex-husband pacified, Henry turned his attention back to England. After months of fighting, Henry and Stephen came to an agreement whereby Henry was acknowledged as Stephen's heir. Plots to kill Henry in favor of Stephen's young son William swirled, and Henry repaired to Normandy.

On October 25, 1154, Stephen of Blois died of a stomach ailment, and Henry II became King of England. Eleanor was crowned Queen by the Archbishop of Canterbury on December 19th of the same year. Through marriage to Henry, in addition to being Duchess of Aquitaine in her own right, Eleanor became Countess of Anjou, Countess of Maine, Duchess of Normandy, Countess of Nantes, Queen of England and Lady of Ireland. She was the most powerful woman in Europe.

❧❧❧

Eleanor and Henry had a fiery, passionate and intemperate marriage. They argued often but also had eight children (William, Henry, Richard, Geoffrey, john, Matilda, Eleanor and Joan). Henry was a tireless philanderer, and one of his by-blows, a son named Geoffrey of York, was raised by Eleanor in the court at Westminster. One wonders how much the queen enjoyed the constant reminder of her husband's infidelity. His affairs with Rosamund Clifford and Annabel de Balliol became public knowledge, which strained their relationship to the breaking point. They were barely on speaking terms by 1166.

❧❧❧

In the early days of their marriage, Henry and Eleanor experienced a great many tests. Aquitaine refused to answer to Henry, only accepting orders from Eleanor, as was its wont. Eleanor and Henry attempted to take possession of Toulouse, claiming inheritance through Eleanor's grandmother, but the effort ended unsuccessfully. Finally, Henry and Thomas

Becket, his former Chancelor and the Archbishop of Canterbury, entered into such a heated feud that the king shouted in 1170,

"Will no one rid me of this turbulent priest?"

Two of his retainers decided that they would do the honors, and they murdered Thomas Becket at the altar. Becket was made a saint, and Henry became a pariah.

☙❧

In France, Louis had finally had his long-hoped-for son with his third wife. His daughter from his second marriage, Marguerite of France, married "Young Henry," the son of Henry and Eleanor. Their daughter, Matilda, married Henry the Lion of Saxony in 1167. Eleanor gathered all of her possessions in England and moved back to Argentan in Normandy, where she spent Christmas with her husband. They agreed to separate during that visit, and when the holiday was over, she left immediately for Poitiers. Henry personally accompanied her there with his army, then left to besiege disloyal vassals nearby. He left Earl Patrick, who was his regional military commander, to be Eleanor's protector. Patrick was slain in a skirmish with more fractious nobles, and Eleanor decided to ransom his son, William Marshal. She was left in control of her own lands once more.

THE COURT OF LOVE

❧

Eleanor had a great deal of influence on culture, but none was greater than that which arose from her stay in Poitiers between 1168 and 1173. While Henry was occupied elsewhere, Eleanor and her daughter Marie established what was called the "Court of Love."

❧

The Court of Love combined the music and poetry of the troubadours, the concept of chivalry and the idea of courtly love into a functional royal court. The court taught the manners and sophistication for which the French court was known in years to come.

❧

According to an account left by Andreas Capellanus in his book *The Art of Courtly Love*, Eleanor, her daughter Marie,

Isabelle of Flanders and Ermengarde, Viscountess of Narbonne, would sit as a tribunal and listen to the complaints of lovers. They would make decisions and rulings in matters of romantic relationships. Among the 21 cases that Capellanus details, one struggled with the question of whether or not true love was possible between a husband and wife. (The judges said it was unlikely.)

⚜

This court had no legal power, and it was most likely a kind of parlor game or silly activity to keep the courtiers busy and entertained. Nevertheless, the impact of the Court of Love was long lasting. One of the troubadours who wrote for Marie de France, Eleanor's daughter, was one Chretién de Troyes, whose works formed the basis of most of the surviving stories of King Arthur and the Knights of the Round Table. Chretién's stories of Sir Lancelot and his love affair with Queen Guinevere have formed one of the most enduring tales in all of western literature. The very nature of the Arthurian tales and the stories of love and loss owe a great deal to Eleanor's Court of Love.

❦ VI ❧

CHAPTER 5 – REBELLION, RANSOM AND RETRIBUTION

*

"What family doesn't have its ups and downs?"

— ELEANOR OF AQUITAINE

REVOLT

❧

In 1173, Eleanor and Henry's youngest son John was preparing to marry the daughter of the Count of Maurienne. As part of the marriage agreement, Henry bequeathed three castles to John and his intended wife, taking it from the inheritance that their eldest son, the Young Henry, expected for himself. Henry II had already been isolated throughout Christendom because of his involvement in the martyrdom of Thomas Becket, and this impingement of his son's inheritance made his popularity plummet even further.

❧

The Young Henry was residing in the court of his father-in-law, Louis VII, the king with whom Henry II had been feuding for years. Young Henry was charming and handsome, and he had a glamorous retinue of knights and hangers-on, but he had few lands. The loss of these three castles was a mortal insult, and his father-in-law and many nobles with something to gain encouraged him to rebel against the king.

⚜

Young Henry traveled to Aquitaine, where his younger brothers Richard and Geoffrey were residing with Eleanor. He appealed to his mother and brothers for assistance, and Eleanor, who was hardly on good terms with her husband, was only too willing join him.

⚜

Geoffrey and Richard were sent to King Louis's court in Paris, and Young Henry and his father-in-law went to work establishing a large and powerful opposition to Henry II. They promised lands and revenues in England and Anjou to the Count of Flanders, the Count of Boulogne, and the Count of Blois. They promised Northumberland to William the Lion, King of the Scots.

⚜

Eleanor encouraged her nobles to join the revolt, and in the spring of 1173, she left Poitiers to join her sons at the court of her former husband. She was apprehended on the road by forces loyal to Henry II, and she was sent to him at his stronghold at Rouen. She was imprisoned and hidden, and for over a year, nobody knew where she was. Henry kept the news of her arrest a complete secret.

⚜

The fighting began in April 1173 when the Count of Flanders

and the Count of Bolougne led their forces in an attack on Normandy from the east, while an attacking force of Bretons march on Normandy from the west. The attack was a failure, and the Count of Bolougne was killed. Louis led his army into Normandy as well, but he was solidly defeated and kicked back out. Meanwhile, William the Lion attacked northern England from his kingdom in Scotland, but he met with no more success than his allies had. Negotiations were tepidly attempted, but Henry II and the Young Henry could not come to terms, so the fighting continued.

⚜

Another of the Young Henry's supporters, the Earl of Leicester, gathered a group of Flemish mercenaries and sailed to England from Normandy, intent upon joining up with some rebellious barons who were opposing Henry there. He was intent upon joining up with Hugh Bigod, the Earl of Norfolk, but was intercepted by the English army as it marched home from defeating William the Lion. Richard de Luci, the leader of the army, demolished the Flemish mercenaries at Fornham and reportedly told Henry II, "It is a bad year for your enemies."

⚜

The fighting stopped for the winter, as was customary in medieval warfare, but resumed in the spring of 1174. David, Earl of Huntingdon, who was William the Lion's younger brother, led an army back into northern England, where he med up with rebel baron William de Ferrers, the Earl of Derby. They put the royal burgh of Nottingham to the torch, and at the same time, Hugh Bigod burned Norwich.

＊＊＊

In July 1174, when Henry II took Eleanor by ship from Barfleur to Southampton. As soon as she set foot in England, she was spirited away to either Winchester Castle or Sarum Castle, where she was imprisoned once again.

＊＊＊

Meanwhile, Henry returned to Canterbury, where he did public penance for his role in the death of Thomas Becket. The next day, William the Lion and his army were surprised and routed by a small loyalist force at the Battle of Alnwick. Henry marched through England, "visiting" each of his enemies' castles and receiving their surrenders in person. At least twenty castles were demolished in England at Henry's command. With one kingdom finally sorted, Henry returned to Normandy, where he forced a settlement onto his sons, who returned to the fold. Blame for the rebellion was placed on Young Henry's advisors and the rebel barons, who "manipulated" the "rash" young princes. Eleanor was also blamed, and it's likely that she was guilty as charged.

IMPRISONMENT

❦

For the next seventeen years, Eleanor languished in prison. She was taken from castle to castle in England, and she became increasingly distant from her sons. This especially pained her where Richard was concerned, for he was always her favorite, and the distance between them was painful for her.

❦

She released on special occasions, such as Christmas, when she would sometimes be able to see her sons. For the most part, though, she was held completely cut off from the rest of the world, with only her jailors and one lady in waiting named Amaria for company. She had no ability to send or receive correspondence and could receive no visitors, which drastically cut down on her ability to plot against her husband... which was, of course, the point of her captivity.

The details of her exact daily life are sketchy at best, and from the few surviving records that remain, it appears that though she was kept in the comfort to which a queen was entitled, and she was treated with courtesy by her keepers, she had few extra luxuries. Eleanor had always been an active woman, a lover of hunting and hawking, and the inability to even go out of doors must have been painful for her.

In Poitiers, the news of her imprisonment was greeted with outrage and grief. The Duchess of Aquitaine was well-loved by the people in her homeland, and they believed that they would never see her again. They were willing, though, to transfer their affection and loyalty to her son, Richard, who took over the rule of Aquitaine in his mother's absence.

Henry took the opportunity of Eleanor's humiliation and disgrace to openly conduct his love affair with Rosamund Clifford, who was his favorite mistress. He had many mistresses, but Rosamund had been the one he'd flaunted in Eleanor's face, possibly trying to goad her into asking for an annulment. His child by Rosamund, named Geoffrey the same as his third son with Eleanor, had even been placed in Eleanor's household while he was a child. Eleanor, though, was more stubborn than Henry had supposed and spiteful to boot. She refused to take public issue with the boy's presence, or with Henry's very public infidelity.

Henry toyed with the idea of repudiating Eleanor and annulling their marriage, which would have been very much supported by several of his vassals, but to do so would have been to lose her vast holdings. Aquitaine and Anjou were not regions to be discarded, and the money that flowed into his coffers from his wife's land was significant. Eleanor was still beautiful and high-spirited, and the risk in annulment also remained that she might make a marriage with a powerful man who might be too much enemy for Henry to resist. Annulment would be too high a risk, and the political fallout among his other alliances would be too drastic, so he turned from that plan.

☙❧

Henry instead tried to force Eleanor to take the veil and become a nun at the abbey of Fontrevaud, which lay within his own territory and therefore would keep her under close watch. He offered her the position of abbess with all of the wealth and power that post contained. If she agreed, her lands would pass to him without question and she would be closed off from the world as surely as if she were still in prison. Eleanor refused. She had too much life within her yet and no vocation, and so she appealed to the Archbishop of Rouen for his assistance. He refused to allow her to be forced into the nunnery and told Henry that if he intended to pursue it, he (the archbishop) would personally appeal to the Pope to annul the marriage and leave Henry exposed to the chance of a militaristic re-marriage by Eleanor as well as the loss of the income from Aquitaine. Henry demurred and left Eleanor as she was.

☙❧

In Eleanor's absence, Rosamund acted as queen. She presided at court at Henry's side, and the Pipe Rolls, the remaining record of Henry II's household expenditures in the period, show that Rosamund was given a huge allowance, nearly three times what was being spent on Eleanor's comfort and maintenance. Henry saw to it that his illegitimate son Geoffrey was elected Bishop of Lincoln in 1176.

❧

That same year, Rosamund died and left the king bereft. Rumors arose that Eleanor had somehow contrived to poison her. Exactly how she would have been able to do this from prison is an open question, but the rumor ran rampant anyway. A more colorful version of the murder tale went that Eleanor had Rosamund put into a bathtub while an old woman cut her arms. Whatever the nature of her death, she was buried with great pomp and majesty at Gadstow Nunnery, to which Henry dedicated a sizeable sum of money.

❧

In 1183, while Eleanor was still in prison, Young Henry and his little brother Geoffrey again rebelled against Henry II. This time, Richard was on his father's side. Henry and Geoffrey tried to ambush Henry II at Limoges, marching with forces sent by King Phillip II of France, who had inherited Louis VII's throne. Henry II ended up besieging Limoge instead, and Young Henry was forced to flee. He wandered aimlessly through Aquitaine, avoiding his father's army and attempting in vain to raise more soldiers for his rebellion. He contracted dysentery and Eleanor, still in prison in England, had a dream in which she saw Young Henry's death.

Realizing that he was in fact dying, Young Henry was over-come with sorrow and remorse for his rebellion. His father's ring was sent to him, and he begged Henry II to show mercy to Eleanor and to his brothers, and he asked his companions to prevail upon Henry II to release her from her captivity. He passed away without knowing if his wishes had been honored.

❦

Thomas of Earley, Archbishop of Wells, broke the news to Eleanor at Sarum Castle. She wrote to Pope Celestine III:

> *"Grief is not very different from illness: in the impetus
> of its fire it does not recognize lords, it does not
> fear colleagues, it does not respect or spare anyone,
> not even itself. Let no one be surprised, then, if the
> power of grief makes the words more harsh, for I
> lament a public loss while the private grief is
> unconsolably rooted in the depths of my spirit."*

❦

King Phillip II notified Henry II that certain lands in Normandy belonged to his half-sister, Margaret, who was the Young Henry's widow. Henry II, though, objected to this and told Phillip that those lands had belonged to Eleanor before her marriage and should return to her after her son's death. Richard was named King of England, which was an essen-tially powerless title, since Henry II was still actually King. (It was the custom among the House of Capet to crown the heirs to the throne before the ruling king died, and Henry II had mimicked this custom, first with the Young Henry and now with Richard I.)

۞

Henry II declared that power would be shifting among his remaining sons. Geoffrey would remain Duke of Brittany, which he held by marriage, and Henry's favorite son John would become the Duke of Aquitaine. Richard refused to give up Aquitaine, and he enjoyed having the power of the duchy.

Furious, Henry II ordered Geoffrey and John to march against Richard and take Aquitaine by force. The war ended in stalemate at the end of 1184, and the family was forced to make peace in England, reaching their tense agreement at Westminster. Richard still refused to hand over Aquitaine, so Henry brought Eleanor to Normandy to plead his case with her favorite son.

۞

Eleanor spent six months in Normandy, renewing her ties with her son while still being in the custody of a watcher assigned by Henry II. She was unable to persuade Richard to acquiesce, and one wonders how hard she really tried. Henry finally threatened to give Normandy and England to Geoffrey. Richard, faced with losing everything, finally handed over control of Aquitaine to Henry.

۞

At this time, Eleanor was living in England, enjoying a bit

more freedom despite the fact that she was still tightly held by Ralph FitzStephen, Henry II's trusted vassal and jailor. She was able to receive visits from her daughters, including Matilda, who was by now very pregnant. Matilda stayed with Eleanor for the duration of her pregnancy, and Eleanor was able to be present at the birth of her grandson, William.

⚜

In 1186, Geoffrey was killed while jousting in a tournament in Paris, and power shifted again.

IN-FIGHTING

❧

John and Richard had very different relationships with their parents. Richard was the apple of Eleanor's eye, and she doted on him. She encouraged his truculent attitude toward his father and his insistence on independent action and power. John, meanwhile, was his father's favorite. Henry was affectionate with John, while he showed little warmth toward Richard. The rift between father and son was deepened by their argument in 1184.

❧

The tensions between the two kings of England were well-known, and the new French king, Phillip Augustus, knew how to exploit them. He cultivated a close relationship with Henry II, despite the fact that he had little actual friendship for the English king. They formed a close alliance despite the disapproval of their barons, especially those in Flanders and Champagne, who held Henry in disfavor. Phillip Augustus and Geoffrey had been close friends, and the French king had done much to try to push Henry to declare Geoffrey his heir instead of Richard. When Geoffrey died, Phillip Augustus's plans came to naught, and he dropped the pretense of friendship with Henry II.

Upon Geoffrey's death, Phillip Augustus demanded that he be given custody of the late prince's children as well as his lands in Brittany. He also insisted that Henry order Richard to withdraw from Toulouse, where Richard and his army were pressuring Phillip Augustus's uncle Raymond. To back up his demands, the French king threatened to invade Normandy if Henry did not comply. He also reopened the demand for lands around the Vexin, a portion of Normandy, which he believed should be given back to Young Henry's widow Margaret, who was Phillip Augustus's sister. The Vexin had been part of Margaret's dowry, and now Phillip Augustus wanted it back. Henry still occupied the Vexin and refused to part with it.

Finally, Phillip Augustus and Henry agreed that Henry could keep the land on the condition that he finally permits Richard to marry Phillip's sister Alys, which had been long discussed but never allowed. Alys, though, was one of Henry's mistresses, his new favorite after the death of Rosamund, and he was loath to give her up. There was some talk that he intended to marry Alys himself, talk that found its way to Eleanor. The true queen fostered a deep hatred for Alys.

The question continued to wrangle until finally Phillip invaded Normandy and Henry counter-attacked. The two armies met in battle at Châteauroux, Phillip Augustus was Henry's liege lord, since Henry was Count of Anjou, which owed fealty to the French crown. The Pope attempted to mediate between the two kings, but without much success. He secured an agreed end to hostility but not a true treaty. The wedge that the French king had long hoped to drive between father and son was now complete.

🕸

Henry called Eleanor to his side, and she once again reigned as queen. He hoped that she could use her influence over Richard to compel him to accept Henry's plans, which involved giving the disputed lands to Henry's favorite, John. If he believed that Eleanor would support him against her favorite, he was woefully misinformed.

🕸

Instead, with his mother's blessing, Richard took his retinue to Paris, where he and Phillip began a long and extremely close friendship. The two young men rode and hunted together, and chronicles state, "Phillip so honored him that every day they ate at the same table, shared the same dish, and at night the bed did not separate them." Their closeness alarmed Henry, who let slip his intention of marrying Alys to John. Upon news of this perfidy – for Alys had been promised to Richard via an official contract – Richard vowed to join with Phillip in his war against Henry when the current peace agreement between the two kings expired.

❧ VII ❧

CHAPTER 6 – PALACE POLITICS

"By the wrath of God, Queen of England."

— ELEANOR OF AQUITAINE

ANOTHER CRUSADE

❦

I t was at this point that war in France was interrupted by war in the Holy Land. In 1187, Jerusalem surrendered to Saladin, and at the fall of the Holy City, cries for a new crusade swept across Europe. Richard, a strong and war-loving fighter, was eager to join, and he announced his intention to take up the cross. In 1188, not to be outdone, Henry II and Richard's beloved Phillip Augustus announced their own intention to join. Taxes were raised to pay for the crusade, and supplies, transports and fighting men were gathered.

❦

Richard was eager to leave, but he was obliged to wait for Henry to finish making arrangements to field his army. With nothing to do, Richard busied himself with crushing enemies in Aquitaine who had supported the transfer of the duchy to John, and then, once that was done, he again attacked Count

Raymond of Toulouse in his eternal quest to claim that territory.

⚜

These attacks strained the truce between Henry and Phillip, and both kings switched their mobilization efforts from crusading to fighting one another. Phillip offered a short-term peace deal so that they could see to the matter of Jerusalem, but Henry rejected this, hoping instead for longer terms. Richard believed that the whole kerfuffle was designed to stall for time and delay the crusade. Henry, who saw that Eleanor was not being helpful to his side, sent her back to prison in England, where she was locked up under the control of William Marshal, whom she had tried to ransom when he was a boy.

⚜

Through all of the struggles in France, Henry II had not yet recognized an heir. Richard was titular King of England, but this was an empty title that could be taken away at a whim by Henry, and it looked likely that this would happen. Richard turned on Henry with a will, and to forestall violence, Phillip called a peace conference in 1188. He publicly offered a generous long-term peace settlement with Henry, allowing all of the territorial demands that Henry had made, on the condition that Henry finally permit the marriage between Richard and Alys.

⚜

The marriage between Richard and Alys would prevent Henry from casting off Eleanor and marrying Alys himself. It would also prevent him from declaring John as his successor and securing that succession by marrying Alys to John. All power turned on the matter of this one dynastic marriage. Henry refused to have his hand forced, and he refused. At that point, Richard publicly demanded to be named as Henry's successor, and when Henry balked, he openly pledged fealty to Phillip in the presence of the entire court.

৩৯৫৩

The Pope, who had reason to want his Crusade to proceed and had no time for this Angevin/Plantagenet quarrel, tried again to secure a peace deal, this time at a conference at La Ferté-Bernard in 1189. Henry was now suffering from a bleeding ulcer, and he knew that he was dying. Stubborn as always, he stuck with his plans and demanded that Phillip pass the marriage contract from Richard to John and made it subtly clear without actually saying that words that he intended to disinherit Richard.

৩৯৫৩

As soon as the period of the current truce expired, as they had pledged to one another, Richard and Phillip attacked Henry at Le Mans. He was surprised but managed to stave off the assault, then made a forced march north to Alençon, which he could use as a springboard to escape into the friend-lier territory of Normandy. His illness was too grave, though, and by now everyone knew that he was dying. Richard and Phillip pursued Henry, winning engagement after engagement, and finally Henry agreed to a compete surrender. Alys would be given up to a guardian, instead of being in Henry's "care," and after the crusade, she would be married to Richard. He also recognized Richard as his heir.

63

In the middle of the conflict, John switched sides and allied with Richard and Phillip. When the news reached Henry, the shock was too much for him to bear, and he died at Chinon on July 6, 1189. He had wanted to be buried at Grandmont Abbey in the Limousin, but because of the hot weather and the fact that embalming was not yet known in Europe, he was instead buried at Fontrevaud Abbey, the same place where he had attempted to force Eleanor to take the veil.

A NEW QUEEN

❦

Eleanor was released from prison immediately upon Henry's death, and she rode to Westminster Abbey, where she received oaths of fealty from many lords and nobles in the name of her son, the new King Richard I. She ruled England in Richard's name, signing her proclamations and edicts as "Eleanor, by the Grace of God, Queen of England." Richard himself finally sailed to England 1189, arriving in Portsmouth on August 13, where he was enthusiastically greeted by his new subjects.

❦

Eleanor, who at 67 years of age was still beautiful and energetic, spent her hours drumming up support for her son. She took her court on the road, traveling through the southern shires. She went from city to city and from castle to castle, and everywhere she went, the nobility were put on notice to obey her commands. She continued to receive oaths of loyalty in Richard's name, and she dispensed justice in courts of law on her son's behalf. She regulated commerce, requiring that uniform weights and measures be used for grain, liquid commodities and cloth. She founded a hospital for the sick and infirm in Surrey, and to the men who had supported Richard's various rebellions against his father, she returned lands that Henry II had confiscated.

◌⊱⊰◌

She sent, with Richard's blessing, orders that all political prisoners who had been put in chains by Henry II should be released on the condition that they swore loyalty oaths to the new king. She relaxed the draconian royal forest laws, and pardoned men who had been declared felons for trespassing or poaching on the king's land. She restrained the sheriffs, who had been riding roughshod over the people with Henry's blessing for many years (similar to the fictional character of the Sheriff of Nottingham in *Robin Hood*, which is set in this time period).

◌⊱⊰◌

She corrected many of her husband's excesses. Many royal heiresses had been taken into custody and held in the king's wardship, and she released these ladies and married them to wealthy young noblemen whose loyalty Eleanor wished to encourage. She also ended a punitive order of Henry's that required religious houses to keep and care for royal horses in case the king's messengers should need relays, or in case the king should wish to arrive and ride. The upkeep of these animals was terribly expensive, and for some poor brotherhoods, it was ruinous. Eleanor corrected that oppression.

66

She was well loved by the people, and many saw her wisdom and kindness and good rule as proof positive that the scandalous rumors of her youth were lies. She was the very image of the wise and caring queen, and the fame of her goodness, sagacity and good works reached the continent.

One person who did not benefits from Eleanor's mercies was Alys of Vexin, Richard's intended bride and the woman who may or may not have been groomed to take Eleanor's place as queen. Eleanor ordered Alys to be held in strict captivity at Winchester. Whatever else became of Alys, Eleanor wanted to be certain it had nothing to do with Richard.

Richard was crowned with great ceremony on September 3, 1189. All women were barred from the ceremony and from the banquet thereafter, except for Eleanor, whose presence was arranged by special invitation. The coronation was lavish and grand, and the amount of money spent was exorbitant.

John, meanwhile, married his cousin, Hawise of Gloucester. He was so eager to obtain his bride's lands that he did not wait for papal dispensation, and as a result, an interdict was placed upon the couple by the Vatican. They were ordered to refrain from sexual intercourse until their marriage was approved. The couple never had any children.

Richard showered his little brother with gifts upon the occasion of his wedding. He gave John the county of Mortain in Normandy and six English counties: Nottinghamshire, Derbyshire, Dorset, Somerset, Devon and Cornwall. The generosity of the gift made it clear that Richard was considering John as his official heir.

⚜

Unfortunately for Richard, the loss of the revenues from the lands he gave to John and the amount he'd spent on his own coronation put him deeply in debt to his old friend and liege lord Phillip Augustus. To repay the debt and to fund his upcoming Crusade, Richard levied punishing taxes on his English citizens and began to sell crown land and public offices for exorbitant prices. His popularity plummeted, and he left England for Normandy, leaving the kingdom in Eleanor's hands.

⚜

Officially, Richard appointed custodians of the realm to rule in his absence. By the time he left for the Crusades, there were two custodians: Hugh de Puiset, Bishop of Durham and Chief Justiciar, and William de Longchamps, Chancellor. De Puiset was responsible for keeping order in the north, and Longchamps in the south. Eleanor was not officially the regent, but by Richard's order, both de Puiset and Longchamps deferred to her, and it was her job to keep the two men, who hated one another, from coming to blows. At the same time, Richard returned the power of Duke of Aquitaine and Count of Poitu to Eleanor. Because she was busy ruling England, she entrusted Aquitaine and Poitu to her deputy and grandson, Otto of Brunswick, son of the Young Henry and Princess Marguerite of France.

❧

Richard returned to Normandy and granted a charter to the Cathedral of Notre-Dame in Rouen at Eleanor's request, "for the weal of his soul and those of his father and mother." The inclusion of Henry II in the bequest indicates that, possibly, Eleanor had begun to warm once again to her late husband. At Christmas, Richard and Phillip met at Nonancourt to plan their Crusade, and at that time, considering the effect that Eleanor and her ladies had on the Second Crusade, they decided to ban all women from accompanying the army. The Pope confirmed this decision with a papal bull.

❧

On February 2, 1190, Richard summoned Eleanor to his side in Normandy. She brought John, Alys, Archbishop Geoffrey and a host of clerics and priests from England. Alys was almost immediately placed back under guard at Rouen. Richard had not yet declared a regency, and as he prepared to go to war with no heir, he needed to put his affairs in order. He had learned from watching John's grasping nature that he could not be trusted, and he forced his brother to swear not to return to England for three years. Eleanor objected, saying that the oath he was requesting was unjust, and though John did swear as he was told, Richard eventually backed down and freed him from his promise. Both Richard and Eleanor would come to regret allowing John the freedom to return to England. Archbishop Geoffrey, Richard's illegitimate half-brother, was also forced to swear to stay away from England for three years. This time, Eleanor did not object.

While the royal family were occupied in Normandy, there was drama with the custodians of the realm. In York, 150 Jews were killed when anti-Semitic violence swept through the town. The Jews sought refuge in Clifford's Tower, but they were locked in and the tower set alight. The perpetrators of this outrage were friends and associates of Bishop de Puiset, and William Longchamps wasted no time in marching on York to set things right. He took the opportunity to issue a warrant for de Puiset's arrest, and only when the bishop bought his freedom with castles and hostages did Longchamps relent. Almost immediately, Longchamps's brother, Osbert, seized de Puiset and imprisoned him. With his rival out of the way, Longchamps moved from Chancellor to acting Justiciar, and at Richard's behest, he was also the papal legate to the court. In the absence of the royal family, he exerted vast power and lived like a king. He even levied taxes on the people to support his extravagant lifestyle.

A NEW BRIDE

※

In France, with the Crusade looming and Richard still unmarried and childless, Eleanor and her son were concerned with the matter of succession. There were three viable heirs to Richard's throne, and none of the options were good. His older brother, Geoffrey, had left behind a young son named Arthur of Brittany, but he was only three years old and was being raised in a hostile court by his mother, Constance. There was John, who was unreliable and greedy, and who Richard did not trust. Last, there was Archbishop Geoffrey, but he was both priest and bastard, and by law could not inherit the throne.

※

There was still the matter of Richard's contracted marriage to Alys. The fact that Alys had been Henry II's lover, and had in fact borne him a son, made her an unsuitable candidate for queen. Any progeny that she bore, even if they were actually

Richard's children, would carry a cloud of doubt about their parentage. The trouble with abandoning Alys was that her brother was King Phillip, Richard's liege lord and former bosom friend, and any repudiation of the princess would enrage Phillip and cause political friction between the two kingdoms.

❧

It was resolved the Richard would find another bride, but that Phillip would not be told until it was too late for him to protest or do anything about it. In Spain, in the kingdom of Navarre, King Sancho VI was a friend to Eleanor. He had written to Henry during Eleanor's captivity, begging for her release, and the troubadour culture of Eleanor's Court of Love had been adopted by his own court. He had a daughter, the 25-year-old virgin Berengaria, whom Richard had met once before and found to be both lovely and charming. She was a meek girl, proper and pious, with no smudges on her reputation and no past that would come back to haunt Richard if she should become queen. Eleanor decided that she would be a perfect choice for Richard's wife, and Richard agreed.

❧

The plan was hatched that when Richard left for Crusade, Eleanor would collect Berengaria and bring her to meet with Richard on Sicily, where he would stop enroute to the Holy Land. This was to be done as subtly as possible, with hopefully no word reaching Phillip. Eleanor was in her late sixties, but she was still quite capable of taking the overland route through the Pyrenees Mountains between France and Spain, and then to bring the princess through the Alps into Italy.

Other ladies of her age would have been daunted, but Eleanor was not most ladies.

❧

Richard and Phillip met up at Vézelay on July 4, 1190 and departed for the Crusades via separate routes. When Richard reached Sicily and the city of Messina, the people there had already had their fill of crusaders, and they locked their gates to him. Their objections meant little to Richard, who easily took Messina anyway and made it his headquarters. He settled in to wait for Eleanor and Berengaria.

❧

While he was there, he learned that his sister, Joanna, the Queen of Sicily, had become a widow, and that Tancred of Lecce had usurped the Sicilian throne. Joanna was a prisoner, and her dowry and all of her lands had been stolen. Phillip had reached Sicily before Richard, and he had already accepted Tancred's hospitality. In fact, Phillip was acting as Joanna's jailer. Richard was furious and demanded his sister's immediate release. Tancred, who had already heard about Richard's fighting prowess – as had all of Europe – was in no hurry to wrangle with the English king, and he released Joanna to her brother immediately.

❧

As Eleanor and Berengaria approached, they stopped off in Milan and Eleanor had a visit with Holy Roman Emperor Henry VI, who was on his way to Rome to be crowned by the Pope. News of her visit with her distant cousin reached Phillip and Tancred, and Phillip began to fill Tancred's head with lies that the Angevins – Richard, Eleanor and Henry VI – were uniting against him, intent on kicking him out of his usurped throne. Tancred believed every word and turned hostile toward Richard, adamantly refusing to part with Joanna's lands. Phillip had heard that Eleanor was bringing Berengaria, and it didn't take a genius to realize why. At his urging, Tancred refused to allow Eleanor and Berengaria's ship to make landfall on Sicily.

⬦⬦⬦

Phillip wrote letters to Tancred filled with dire warnings, and these letters were re-routed to Richard instead. Armed with the proof of his former friend's betrayal, Richard was able to convince Tancred that he'd been deceived, and in return for Richard acknowledging Tancred as King of Sicily, Tancred would return Joanna's lands to her control. The two kings agreed that Tancred's infant daughter would marry Arthur of Brittany, whom Richard now named as his heir should he die childless in the Crusade. They exchanged kingly gifts, with Richard giving Tancred a sword that was supposed to be King Arthur's Excalibur, which had recently been found in a grave in Glastonbury. Tancred gave Richard nineteen ships and with full crew complement.

⬦⬦⬦

Phillip, meanwhile, had become besotted with Joanna, and Richard had no intention of allowing his vulnerable sister to be dishonored by a relationship with the very married King of France. He appropriated the priory of La Bagnara on the coast of Calabria and ensconced his sister there. Phillip could not reach her, and Joanna was safe.

74

Richard met Eleanor and Berengaria with his own ship and brought them to La Bagnara, where there was a great celebration to welcome the queen and the princess she had brought for her son. Berengaria was a meek and subservient woman, and she readily accepted the position of Eleanor's subordinate, even though as Richard's wife she could easily have taken Eleanor's place in the power structure of the royal family. Instead, she simply obeyed, and after the celebration, and after Eleanor's reunion with her daughter Joanna (the first time in fourteen years they had seen one another), Richard took his mother with him back to Messina.

❧ VIII ❧
CHAPTER 7 – THE THIRD CRUSADE

"He has done serious things, but you can most certainly expect more serious soon."

— ELEANOR OF AQUITAINE

THE END OF FRIENDSHIP

※

Richard confronted Phillip about the lies he had been telling Tancred, and Phillip in return accused Richard of faithlessness and breach of contract. He knew full well that the king of England had no intention of marrying his sister, Alys. In the presence of nobles and courtiers for both kings, Richard publicly revealed his reason for refusing Alys now: she had been his father's paramour and had born Henry II a bastard child.

※

Phillip was aghast and refused to believe the allegation. Eleanor helpfully provided witnesses who could attest to the truth of what Richard said, and in the public shame that ensued, Phillip had no choice but to release Richard from the marriage contract. The two kings signed a treaty, and Richard was obliged to pay a fine for breach of contract, and Richard graciously restored Alys's dowry lands and castles back to her.

He was now free to marry Berengaria, but because it was now Lent and no marriages could be solemnized within the Church, Phillip demanded that Richard wait and marry her when the party reached Acre in the Holy Land. Women had already been banned from accompanying the crusaders, and that meant that Berengaria would not be allowed to go to Acre, not for a wedding or any other reason. Richard balked. Finally Phillip left in a rage, and the two formerly fast and intimate friends were no longer even on speaking terms.

⚜

Eleanor was receiving letters from England detailing the Longchamps's abuses of power, and she grew more and more concerned about the situation. She finalized the wedding arrangements for her son and his Spanish princess, and she left Berengaria in Queen Joanna's capable hands. This was fortuitous, because the two women – Joanna and Berengaria – had formed a close friendship during their stay at La Bagnara, and they would remain close for the rest of their lives. Eleanor convinced Richard to issue a mandate sending Walter of Coutances, the Archbishop of Rouen, to go to England and take control of the situation. Coutances was an old and loyal retainer and he outranked Longchamps. He was also no friend of Longchamps, and he had already counselled John to raise baronial support against the out-of-control Bishop of Durham. Coutance left immediately for England, and Eleanor returned to Normandy to monitor the situation.

⚜

Joanna and Berengaria sailed ahead of Richard, headed for

the Holy Land despite the papal bull. Their ship foundered in Cyprus, where the royal ladies were beset and threatened by the king of that island, Isaac Comnenus. Richard took Cyprus and rescued his sister and his bride-to-be, and on May 12, 1191, Richard and Berengaria were married. She was almost immediately crowned Queen of England, and some of Eleanor's lands in Aquitaine were given to Berengaria as a gift. The gift was in name only, however, as they carried with them the proviso that no power or revenue from those lands would actually pass to Berengaria until after Eleanor's death.

CRUSADE IN THE HOLY LAND, CHAOS IN ENGLAND

☙❧

Richard and his fleet arrived at Acre on June 5, 1191, to find the city under siege by the Crusaders attempting to take it back from the Saracens. The siege had been pressed by Guy de Lusignan, the King of Jerusalem, for two years without success. Richard, with his energy and military genius, arrived with fresh troops and by July 12, the city fell. Richard was at the forefront of the fighting, despite the fact that he had contracted malaria. The Saracen leader Saladin was so impressed with Richard's fortitude and skill that he sent him gifts of fruit. In response, Richard sent Saladin an African slave. The two leaders never met in person, but they held one another in high esteem.

☙❧

When Acre fell, Richard moved Joanna and Berengaria into the royal palace there. His standard was flown from the roof, but alongside it was that of Duke Leopold of Austria, who had done little to nothing to win the day. Annoyed and intemperate, Richard pulled down Leopold's standard and tossed it into the moat, following it with disparaging words about its owner. Leopold was mortally insulted and withdrew his troops from the entire Crusade.

⚜

Richard made a tactical error in dealing with the enemy prisoners. In revenge for the slaughter of Knights Templar and Knights Hospitaler at the fall of Jerusalem, he told Saladin, unless the Saracens came to terms within one week, released all Christian prisoners and gave up the True Cross, Richard would have ever Saracen prisoner taken outside the walls of Acre and put to death. Saladin refused. Despite the pleas of other Crusaders to show mercy, Richard kept his word, and up to 3,000 Turkish men, women and children were beheaded in the field outside the city. The atrocity is still remembered in the Middle East and is one of the evils of the West that modern Islamists point to as reason for their current jihad. Memories are long in that part of the world.

⚜

Richard's successes made Phillip furious, and since he, too, had fallen prey to malaria, Phillip advised Richard that he was too ill to continue and would be returning to France. Richard, contemptuous, let him go without a word. Phillip's real purpose was revenge – he was intent upon going back to France and undermining Richard's power base there.

⚜

When Eleanor reached Normandy, she took up residence at

Rouen and waited to hear back from Walter of Coutances, who had traveled to England and found the political situation in turmoil. John had taken the advice to stir up the barons to heart and had started a revolt against William Longchamp, and he had taken the royal castles at Tickhill and Nottingham by force. Seeing Longchamps' moment of weakness, Roger Mortimer chose that moment to launch a rebellion along the Welsh border as well. Longchamps was fighting a two-front war, and John had learned of Longchamps's support for Richard naming Arthur of Brittany as his heir. As a result, John was enraged and wanted nothing so much as Longchamps' destruction.

❦

It was into this maelstrom that Walter of Coutances stepped at Eleanor and Richard's behest. He began to act as a sort of mediator between John and the Chancellor Longchamps. He was equitable and fair, because he believed that Longchamps was acting in the king's best interests, which was debatable. John was by all appearances going to be the next king, and he himself had begun the rumor that Richard would never return from the Crusade. The barons of England would not accept Arthur of Brittany as their ruler, and because John had opposed Longchamps, his popularity was ascendant. He would be the barons' choice.

❦

A settlement was finally reached by the end of July. John had to give up claim to the castles and towns he had taken, and Longchamps's power was truncated. With false penitence, Longchamps sought to ally himself with John by supporting his claim to the throne over Arthur of Brittany's. John was unconvinced and continued to plot against the Chancellor. It was soon very apparent that John had designs upon the crown itself.

৩১৩

On August 22, Richard left Acre and led his army toward Jerusalem. He was harried by the Muslim forces all along the way, but in spite of this, and despite his supplies running short, he managed to reach Ascalon by the end of the month. He went on to defeat Saladin at the plains of Arsuf and took Jaffa two days later. The crusade was a wild success until Richard again fell ill, this time with a combination of malaria and dysentery. Several of his main supporters had died in the fighting, and he himself was ill for several weeks, but he obsessively insisted on continuing the fight.

৩১৩

While the fighting was going on in England and in the Holy Land, the king's bastard half-brother Geoffrey was consecrated as Bishop of York while he was in Tours, and he prepared to travel to England, disregarding his oath to stay away for three years. Longchamps was determined to keep Geoffrey out of England. He asked for help from the Duke of Flanders to keep him on the continent, but Geoffrey slipped through his net and made landfall at Dover. He was met there by Longchamps's sister, Richent, and several knights. She was the wife of the castellan of Dover, and they insisted that Geoffrey take an oath of fealty to the King and the chancellor. Geoffrey refused, then ran to the priory of St. Martin at Dover to take refuge. The sanctuary was violated by the Richent's knights, and he was dragged bodily from the very

85

altar and through the mud until he was at last thrown into the dungeon at Dover Castle.

છ૪જ

This violation of the laws of church and common decency outraged the people of England, and it echoed back to Thomas Becket's martyrdom at the hands of Henry II's knights. They lionized Geoffrey and blamed Longchamps for the treatment he had received, and while the Chancellor had nothing to do with his sister's rash actions, he was unable to convince anyone that he was innocent. He released Geoffrey, but not before the Bishop of Lincoln excommunicated the Castellan of Dover and his wife, as well as the knights who had seized Geoffrey from the priory. Geoffrey rode in a triumphant procession through London and Longchamps had to take refuge in Windsor Castle.

છ૪જ

John chose to capitalize on Longchamps's troubles and set himself up in the public eye as the champion of the wronged and the oppressed. He gathered together the Chancellor's many enemies, including Hugh de Puiset and Geoffrey of York – and brought them with him as he marched to Reading. Once there, he issued writs assembling the Great Council. Longchamps didn't dare appear there, and when his supporters all deserted him, he fled to the Tower of London and shut himself inside for protection.

છ૪જ

At the Great Council, Longchamps was essentially tried for abuse of power and very nearly was accused of treason. It was agreed that he should be removed from office. John brought his troops to London, where he granted the people of the town the right to self-government under an elected mayor, which they had been requesting for years. At this moment, Coutances produced letters of patent from Queen Eleanor providing him the authority of papal mandate, and he was made head of a council of regency and immediately seized all of Longchamps' possessions.

⚜

Longchamps fled to Dover Castle and tried to escape the country disguised as a woman. Unfortunately for his escape plans, his disguise was discovered by a lusty fisherman, and Longhcamps was apprehended. John permitted him to go into exile in France.

⚜

With the hated Chancellor gone, John set about solidifying his grip on the country. He traveled all around the kingdom on a glad-handing tour, making himself known to all classes and manner of men as Richard's heir. He presided over courts and dispensed justice as if he were already crowned, and he wooed the commoners with lavish gifts and displays. The barons were not impressed, for they knew how untrustworthy he was, and that there was always a chance that Richard would still return. Nobody wanted to be on Richard the Lionheart's bad side, but nobody wanted to be on John's bad side, either, so the barons ingratiated themselves to him anyway.

⚜

Longchamps went straight to Eleanor with his grievances,

which were many. If he expected her support, he was disappointed, for she approved of his dismissal. She hoped to keep him from proceeding to Paris to stir up trouble there, but she was unable to prevent it, and Longchamps did exactly that. He met with two cardinals from Rome and prevailed upon them to intercede with Coutances on his behalf. They went to Eleanor to begin their efforts, but she refused to meet with them. She worried that they might actually have been sent by Phillip, since she still was holding Alys prisoner. The Normans at Gisor Bridge raised the drawbridge against the cardinals and prevented them from entering without the queen's permission. They threatened her with excommunication, but Eleanor was unmoved, and finally the cardinals slunk back to Paris in a snit.

❧❦❧

The cardinals, once they were safely in Paris, excommunicated the seneschal of Rouen where Eleanor was staying and placed all of Normandy under interdict, being careful to explicitly exclude Eleanor from the ban. Longchamps excommunicated the entire regency council in England except for John, and the bishops of England excommunicated Longchamp and placed his diocese of Ely under a revenge interdict. It was a worrisome time for the loyal and devout common folk in those regions whose access to Church sacraments was severed. Geoffrey was finally enthroned as Archbishop of York, but Hugh de Puiset, who had wanted the post for himself, refused to attend out of jealousy. Geoffrey therefore excommunicated him, too. A general revolt by the clergy in York resulted, but it all ended in stalemate.

JERUSALEM IS LOST

❧

In October, Joanna and Berengaria joined Richard in Jaffa, and he found the strength to press on toward Jerusalem. While he had been out of action, his allies had reached a truce with Saladin's brother, Safadin, saying that if Richard assaulted Jerusalem, they would not help him. Nobody bothered to tell Richard that he would be attacking alone.

❧

Richard tried to reach a bargain with Saladin, offering his sister's hand in marriage to Safadin, hoping that they could rule jointly as King and Queen of Jerusalem on the condition that Christians would be allowed to visit the holy sites within the city. This looked like a promising compromise until Joanna very loudly, very publicly and very firmly proclaimed that she would rather die than marry a Saracen.

In December, Richard reached Beit-Nuba, twelve miles from Jerusalem. Severe weather prevented him from assaulting the Holy City, and he spent Christmas at Latrum, within sight of the city walls, with Joanna, Berengaria and King Guy of Jerusalem. It was then that he learned that his allies had deserted him, and his rage was epic.

Phillip returned home to Paris at this point to a hero's welcome, and he began to hint that he had left the Crusade because of Richard's arrogance and treachery, and that his illness had been because the English king had poisoned him. Eleanor knew that these pretenses were being put forward as a way to excuse Phillip from keeping the truce he'd signed with Richard and to take revenge for the insult to Alys. She ordered that all of her family's castles along the border with Phillip's lands be repaired and strengthened, and that their garrisons should be fully manned. In January, Phillip attacked, but he was repulsed. He then demanded the return of his sister, but Eleanor, who had not been given instruction on what to do with her prisoner by Richard, refused.

It was at this moment that news of John's efforts to secure the throne for himself reached France. Phillip sent overtures of friendship to John, offering all of Richard's continental lands in return for John's agreement to marry Alys, himself, and to return the border town of Gisors to France. John, although he had already married Hawise, agreed, and he prepared to come to France to pay homage to his new liege lord with an army of mercenaries.

❧

Eleanor found out about it all, and she returned to England before John could raise his army. She arrived just in time to keep her troublesome son from boarding his own ships. Eleanor convened four meetings of the Great Council to remind the barons of their vows of allegiance to Richard, and made every one of them re-swear their oaths. Then, with the newly sworn nobles and Coutances at her side, she told John that she would confiscate all of his castles and all of his lands if he dared to go to France. John, severely outmatched, backed down.

❧

In France, Phillip's hands were tied. It was against the Truce of God to attack the lands of an absent Crusader, so none of his own barons would raise forces against Richard. Eleanor took advantage of Phillip's hesitation by fortifying all of her towns and castles against attack, even in England. She toured her lands and saw the misery that had been caused by the dueling excommunications, and she prevailed upon Coutances to lift his interdict and allow Longchamps to return to England to act in his capacity as bishop, but not as chancellor. She then asked Hugh de Puiset to travel to Rome to get the cardinals to lift their interdict on Normandy, but he refused to go until Geoffrey lifted the interdict that had been levied against him. Eleanor worked with the quarreling priests, who were all behaving like errant toddlers, and ultimately was able to get the various interdicts and excommunications lifted by appealing directly to the Pope.

The barons were deeply unhappy that Longchamps had returned, and they asked for John's assistance in ridding themselves of him. John would not help because, as he very blatantly put it, he was in need of money. They provided the necessary funds.

The barons were deeply unhappy that Longchamps had returned, and they asked for John's assistance in ridding themselves of him. John would not help because, as he very blatantly put it, he was in need of money. They provided the necessary funds.

Eleanor was alarmed by the re-arming of her son, and she sent word to Richard that Phillip had been tempting John into treason, that John had been responding, and that it was time for Richard to come home. She enticed John and the barons to join her in writing a letter to Longchamps, advising him to return to France, which he did. Phillip, meanwhile, had fomented a rebellion among Richard's southernmost vassals, but their little fire was stamped out by King Sancho of Navarre, Richard's father-in-law, and Élie de la Celle, the faithful seneschal of Gascony.

Richard was in dire straits. He had toiled and labored, bled and fought, but he was no nearer to his goal of retaking Jerusalem than when he had started. Worse, he once again fell ill, and it was feared that he would die. He received his mother's letters, along with a gift of fruit and snow from Saladin, and resolved to go home. He concluded a peace treaty with Saladin and departed for Sicily. He would never see Jerusalem.

His ship sailed from Acre on October 9, and he had sent

Joanna and Berengaria on a different ship ahead of him. Richard's return was anticipated in the late autumn, but the King did not appear. Winter came, and still there was no news of him. Rumors began to circulate that Phillip and John had somehow colluded to bring the king to grief, and Eleanor held her winter court at Westminster in great concern. Joanna and Berengaria safely reached Rome, but there was still no news of Richard.

༺✦༻

In January 1193, a letter arrived bearing the bad news. Richard had been stopped on his return march home and had been imprisoned by Leopold of Austria, the duke whose standard Richard had torn down at Acre.

❧ IX ❧
CHAPTER 8 – RANSOM

"Grief is not very different from illness: in the impetus of its fire it does not recognize lords, it does not fear colleagues, it does not respect or spare anyone, not even itself."

— ELEANOR OF AQUITAINE

TO JAIL A KING

෨෬෯

Eleanor was heartbroken at the news of Richard's kidnapping. She wanted to go to Austria herself to negotiate for his release, but with John's grasping behavior and the kingdom in disarray and under threat from Phillip, she had no choice but to stay. She saw her son's troubles as God's punishment for her sins, and she was overcome with anxiety for Richard's wellbeing. She began to waste away and sought solace from the nuns at Fontrevaud, whose prayers she asked for twice.

෨෬෯

The news of Richard's predicament was not made public knowledge, partially because the Austrians had a reputation for barbarity that would have cast his survival into doubt in the minds of the people. It was unclear where in Austria Richard was being held prisoner, so she sent envoys to the Holy Roman Emperor, entreating him for news. Joanna and

Berengaria, fearing for their safety if they traveled farther, stayed in Rome under the protection of the Pope, who was aghast at the violation of the Truce of God. He excommunicated Duke Leopold and informed Phillip that he would face a similar fate if he dared to intrude onto Richard's lands.

※

Eleanor did the only thing she could. She traveled to England and took control of Richard's realm. She had the support of the regency council and the people, with whom she was respected and beloved.

※

John behaved as badly as could be anticipated at the news that his brother had been kidnapped. He made many promises to the barons and people in England, then scurried across the Channel to Normandy to proclaim himself Richard's heir and to start making promises there. The Norman lords received him guardedly, so he continued on to Paris, where he was given a warm welcome. He paid homage to Phillip for all of the lands his family held on the continent, including Normandy, Aquitaine, Poitu and Anjou. There is some indication that he might have offered England, too. He and Phillip agreed to do everything they could to keep Richard in chains.

※

In February 1193, the Holy Roman Emperor Henry VI and Leopold reached an agreement on splitting the ransom that had been demanded for Richard, and the King was turned over to the Emperor. He was imprisoned by the Emperor at

Ochsenfurt. Various German princes objected to the treatment of the Crusader king, but the Emperor silenced them by threatening to just execute Richard for his supposed crimes. The English king was then brought to the Diet at Speyer to answer for those charges, but he defended himself so well that the Emperor, instead of convicting him, instead bestowed the kiss of peace. It was at the Diet that Hubert Walter, Bishop of Salisbury, Richard's loyal vassal, encountered his king. Richard provided him with letters for his mother and instructions to the Queen that Hubert, whom Richard liked well for his elegance and handsome face, should be nominated to become the next Archbishop of Canterbury.

☙❧

Eleanor was horrified to learn of Richard's captivity by the Emperor, whose reputation was horrid in the extreme. She wrote to the Pope, who had failed to do more than excommunicate Leopold and threaten Phillip despite his promises to intercede on Richard's behalf. Eleanor's letters, angrily upbraiding him for his lack of action in assistance of a crusader, exist to this day. The letters are heartfelt and in places heartbreaking:

☙❧

> *"Who may allow me to die for you, my son? Mother
> of mercy, look upon a mother so wretched, or else,
> if your Son, an unexhausted source of mercy,
> requires from my son the sins of the mother, then
> let Him exact complete vengeance on me, for I am
> the only one to offend, and let Him punish me, for
> I am the irreverent one. Do not let Him smile
> over the punishment of an innocent person. Let*

He who now bruises me take up His hand and
slay me. Let this be my consolation – that in
burdening me with grief, He does not spare me..."

❧

The sad truth was that Pope Celestine III was eighty-seven years old and too afraid of repercussions to really risk angering the Emperor. The Papacy and the Holy Roman Empire had a long history of enmity, and it would take little to incite the proud Emperor to strike violently at the Pope, who was in no position to repel the blow.

REBELLION

❧

J ohn returned to England and declared that Richard was dead. Nobody believed him. He marched with an army of mercenaries to London and tried to convince Eleanor that Richard would never return and he should be made king. She was unmoved, and John was forced to retreat to Windsor Castle. Eleanor retained control of England and ordered her men to kill any of John's mercenaries they could find.

❧

Phillip, meanwhile, invaded Normandy. He laid siege to Rouen and demanded the return of his sister Alys. The seneschal of Rouen, Robert de Beaumont, the Earl of Leicester, advised him that he could not release her, but he would be happy to let Phillip come in and visit if he came unarmed and alone. The threat of imprisoning Phillip, perhaps even to trade him for Richard, was not lost on him, and he withdrew his siege and returned to Paris.

⚜

Phillip of France offered Henry VI a sizeable amount of money to keep Richard in chains, but Henry had no wish to increase Phillip's power, because he wanted to rule over all of Europe's princes himself. Instead he set a ransom amount of 100,00 silver marks for Richard's release. This was equal to twice England's annual revenue, the equivalent today of several million pounds. He also wanted hostages to be selected from the noble houses of England and Normandy.

⚜

The money was to be raised and entrusted to Eleanor. As a token of good will in return for the agreement Richard and Henry had reached, Richard was now treated as an honored guest. He was allowed to hold court and attend to the matter of running his realm, orchestrated through correspondence with Eleanor. Eleanor went to work raising the ransom, both in England and in Aquitaine. The Pope finally got involved and threatened to place all of England under interdict if Richard's subjects failed to raise the amount of money needed to win their king's freedom.

⚜

While he was waiting, Richard made arrangements with Henry VI that would have put them into a strong position of alliance against the rest of Europe. The ransom was raised and Eleanor personally delivered the funds. Phillip, horrified, sent word to John in England:

102

"Look to yourself. The Devil is loosed!"

※

The game wasn't over yet. John and Phillip offered Henry VI an even larger amount of money if he rejected the ransom, and when Eleanor arrived in Germany, she was informed that the deal had changed. In order to overcome her traitorous son's counteroffer, the entirety of England must be pledged to Henry. The terms were humiliating, but Eleanor would do anything to get Richard back. She agreed, and Richard was released.

※

Eleanor and Richard returned to England, where John was called before the king to account for his behavior. He was chastised and punished, but not removed from the succession, for Richard still had no issue and Eleanor interceded on his behalf. A new coronation was staged for Richard, and then he and Eleanor returned to Normandy to see about reconquering the lands that Phillip had taken.

※

Neither of them would ever see England again.

꙰ X ꙰

CHAPTER 9 – SUNSET

"In all things the Lord has turned cruel to me and attacked me with the harshness of His hand."

— ELEANOR OF AQUTAINE

FORGIVENESS AND GRIEF

෴

Richard set about retaking all of the land that he had lost to his erstwhile friend Phillip. He was swift and terrible in his retribution, and Phillip was defeated time and time again. At the Battle of Fretéval, Richard dealt Phillip such a jarring rout that the French king was obliged to flee so swiftly that he left behind his treasure, his archives, his battle plans and even his royal seal, all of which were recovered by his enemy. Phillip himself hid in a chapel by the side of the road until Richard's forces had passed.

෴

Richard continued on to quell a rebellion in Aquitaine that Phillip had teased into being, and in his final battle there, he captured some 300 knights and 40,000 foot soldiers. The Church intervened, and in 1195, Richard and Philip reached a treaty.

In April 1199, Richard died of a gangrenous arm wound suffered while besieging another rebellion vassal, and before he passed, he named his brother John as the heir to his throne. Richard was buried at Fontrevaud Abbey beside his father.

Eleanor's last great act upon the international stage came when a treaty between King Phillip II and King John agreed that Phillip's son Louis would be married to one of John's nieces, daughters of his sister, the Queen of Castile. Eleanor was entrusted with choosing the daughter who would be the bride.

At the advanced age of 77, Eleanor left Poitiers en route to Castile. She was attacked and kidnapped by Hugh IX of Lusignan, who had lost his lands to Henry II and demanded them back. Eleanor was too tired to argue and returned them forthwith, and she was allowed to continue on her way.

The elderly queen crossed the mountains and through Navarre and Castile, where she selected the younger daughter, Blanche, to be the bride. She stayed for two months in Castile, then began to ride back with her granddaughter at her side. They rode in short bursts to the Loire valley, where she entrusted her granddaughter to the care of the Archbishop of Bordeaux, who escorted her the rest of the way to her wedding.

☙❧

In 1201, war broke out between Phillip and John. She declared her support for John, then learned that her grandson Arthur of Brittany, 15 years old, was leading an army into Poitiers. She reached the castle before him, and he besieged her until John came and beat him back. She returned to Fontrevaud and took the veil.

☙❧

Eleanor of Aquitaine died in 1204 and was laid to rest beside her husband and son. She had outlived all but two of her children. She would never outlive her legend.